ROCKS: The Hard Facts

EROSION AND WEATHERING

Willa Dee

PowerKiDS
press.

New York

Published in 2014 by The Rosen Publishing Group, Inc.
29 East 21st Street, New York, NY 10010

First Edition

Editor: Jennifer Way
Book Design: Kate Vlachos
Photo Research: Katie Stryker

Photo Credits: Cover Alan Majchrowicz/Photolibrary/Getty Images; p. 4 Lissandra Melo/Shutterstock.com; p. 6 Grant Dixon/Lonely Planet Images/Getty Images; p. 7 (left) Mariia Savoskula/Shutterstock.com; p. 7 (right) Govert Nieuwland/Shutterstock.com; p. 8 electra/Shutterstock.com; pp. 9, 18 Darren J. Bradley/Shutterstock.com; p. 10 Nancy Bauer/Shutterstock.com; p. 11 Perspectives/Getty Images; p. 12 Maxim Petrichuk/Shutterstock.com; p. 13 (left) Joshua Raif/Shutterstock.com; p. 13 (right) jeremkin/iStock Vectors/Getty Images; p. 14 Melpomene/Shutterstock.com; p. 15 (left) Konstantin Yolshin/Shutterstock.com; p. 15 (right) Jorge Moro/Shutterstock.com; p. 16 Nagel Photography/Shutterstock.com; p. 17 Arena Photo UK/Shutterstock.com; p. 19 kojihirano/Shutterstock.com; p. 20 scubaluna/Shutterstock.com; p. 21 Pecold/Shutterstock.com; p. 22 Jason Patrick Ross/Shutterstock.com.

Publisher's Cataloguing Data

Dee, Willa.
Erosion and weathering / by Willa Dee.
   p. cm. — (Rocks: the hard facts)
Includes index.
ISBN 978-1-4777-2904-5 (library binding) — ISBN 978-1-4777-2993-9 (pbk.) —
ISBN 978-1-4777-3063-8 (6-pack)
1. Erosion — Juvenile literature. 2. Weathering — Juvenile literature. I. Title.
QE570.D44 2014
551.3—dc23

Manufactured in the United States of America

CPSIA Compliance Information: Batch #W14PK4: For Further Information contact Rosen Publishing, New York, New York at 1-800-237-9932

CONTENTS

EARTH'S CHANGING SURFACE

Natural features, or **landforms**, cover Earth's surface. All over Earth, you can find tall mountains, wide deserts, low valleys, deep canyons, running rivers, and still lakes. Oceans and seas divide Earth's **continents**, while beaches and cliffs form Earth's coastlines.

The rocks at the bottom of Niagara Falls are smooth because the water wears away their rough edges.

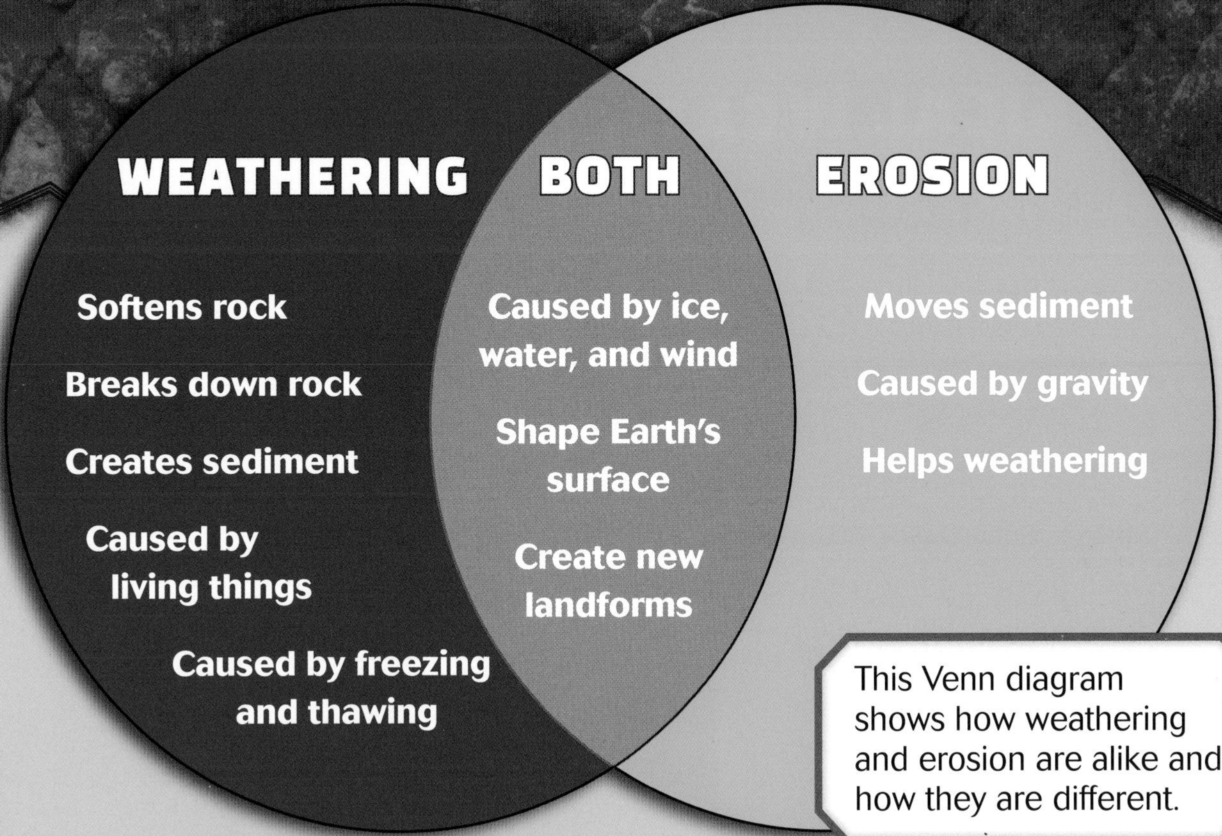

WEATHERING

Softens rock

Breaks down rock

Creates sediment

Caused by living things

Caused by freezing and thawing

BOTH

Caused by ice, water, and wind

Shape Earth's surface

Create new landforms

EROSION

Moves sediment

Caused by gravity

Helps weathering

This Venn diagram shows how weathering and erosion are alike and how they are different.

It may seem like these natural features never change. However, Earth's surface is always changing! Most changes happen very slowly. Over many years, different natural forces can wear down rock and break it into smaller pieces called sediment. This process is called weathering. Erosion is what happens when ice, water, wind, or **gravity** picks up sediment and moves it to another place.

PHYSICAL WEATHERING

Earth's natural forces break down rocks. When this happens without changing the rocks' **mineral** makeup, it is called physical weathering.

One example is when water seeps into the cracks in a rock. If the temperature drops, the water will freeze and **expand**.

Growing plants can also cause physical weathering. When a plant's roots grow in the cracks of a rock, the pressure of the growing roots forces the rock to break apart.

The Sahara Desert can be 50° F (28° C) colder at night than it is during the day. This change in temperature changes rocks.

The ice that forms in the cracks presses against the rock and causes more cracks. When the ice melts, the water goes farther into the new cracks. Over time, this process can break rocks apart.

In deserts, rocks get very hot during the day and very cold at night. These quick changes in temperature put stress on the rock. The rocks' outer layers start to peel off in thin sheets.

CHEMICAL WEATHERING

Rocks can also break down because of **chemical** changes to their minerals. This is called chemical weathering.

Oxidation is one kind of chemical weathering. This happens when oxygen in air **reacts** with iron in rocks. Oxidation makes rocks weak, which helps them break down more easily.

Acid rain can also dissolve rock. Acid rain forms when rainwater mixes with pollution. Acid rain has dissolved the sandstone in this picture.

Oxidation has turned this sandstone red. You can see little red rocks on the ground because oxidation breaks rocks.

Water also causes chemical weathering. Minerals in rocks can **absorb** water, causing them to expand. This weakens the rock. When water reacts with minerals such as feldspar, it can turn rock into clay. Substances **dissolved** in water can also react with minerals in rock. Carbon dioxide and rainwater can react to form an acid. This acid can dissolve limestone.

EROSION BY WATER

Moving water is one of the forces that causes erosion. When it rains, water that is not absorbed by soil flows over the ground. The rainwater picks up loose soil and rock **particles** and carries them away. On hills and mountains, gravity pulls the rainwater, carrying rock particles downward.

When sediment lands in the Mississippi River's channel, it changes the river's path to the Gulf of Mexico. Over 5,000 years, this process has moved the coast of Louisiana 15 to 50 miles (25–80 km) south.

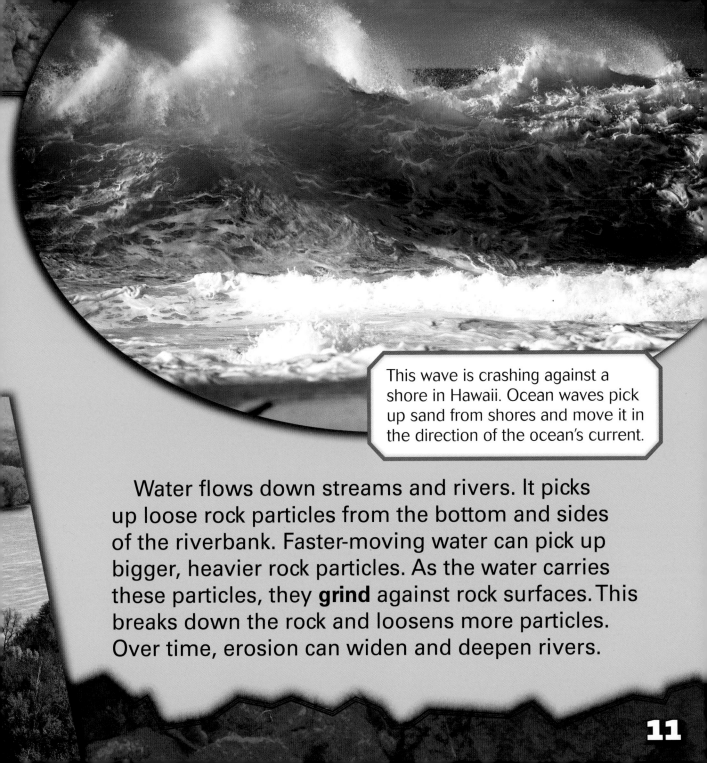

This wave is crashing against a shore in Hawaii. Ocean waves pick up sand from shores and move it in the direction of the ocean's current.

Water flows down streams and rivers. It picks up loose rock particles from the bottom and sides of the riverbank. Faster-moving water can pick up bigger, heavier rock particles. As the water carries these particles, they **grind** against rock surfaces. This breaks down the rock and loosens more particles. Over time, erosion can widen and deepen rivers.

OTHER EROSION

Wind is another force that causes erosion. As it blows, wind picks up loose particles of rock. The particles wind carries can blow against rock surfaces and wear them down. This is called abrasion.

Glaciers are masses of ice that form from snow that does not melt.

Wind is eroding the land in this desert by blowing the sand to another place.

Above: This picture shows the Perito Moreno glacier, in Argentina. It is 3 miles (5 km) wide and has an average height of 240 feet (73 m)! *Left*: This diagram shows how glaciers wear away rocks. As gravity moves the glacier downhill, the glacier carries rock with it.

Gravity

ROCK

GLACIER

Gravity pulls on glaciers, causing them to move slowly downhill. As the glaciers move, pieces of rocks frozen into the ice move with them. Rock pieces frozen into the moving glacier also scrape against the rocks stuck in the ground. This causes more rock to be broken apart as the glacier moves.

SEDIMENT AND SOIL

This person is planting squash plants in soil. Soil has minerals in it that help plants grow.

When rock breaks down, it forms sediment. Pieces of sediment can be as large as boulders. Sediment can also be as small as pebbles or sand. It can even be as tiny as **microscopic** grains of sand, clay, or silt.

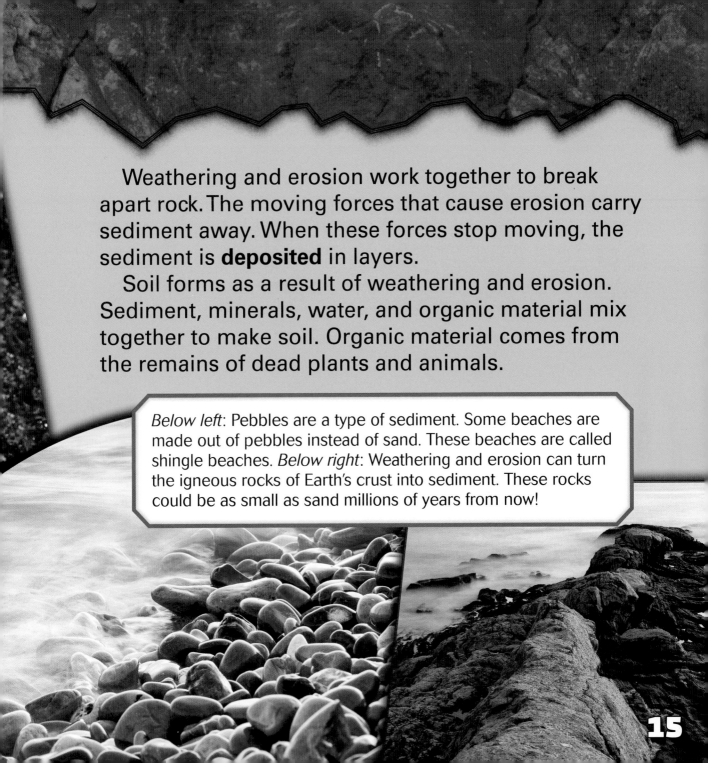

Weathering and erosion work together to break apart rock. The moving forces that cause erosion carry sediment away. When these forces stop moving, the sediment is **deposited** in layers.

Soil forms as a result of weathering and erosion. Sediment, minerals, water, and organic material mix together to make soil. Organic material comes from the remains of dead plants and animals.

Below left: Pebbles are a type of sediment. Some beaches are made out of pebbles instead of sand. These beaches are called shingle beaches. *Below right*: Weathering and erosion can turn the igneous rocks of Earth's crust into sediment. These rocks could be as small as sand millions of years from now!

Over time, sediment deposited by erosion can become rock. When wind or water slows down enough, the sediment it carries is deposited in a layer. Moving wind or water can deposit many layers of sediment in the same place. Layers of sediment can build up over many years.

These tall rock formations in Utah's Bryce Canyon National Park are called hoodoos. They were formed by water erosion.

Monument Valley is a part of the Colorado Plateau that has several buttes in it. A butte is a hill with vertical sides and a flat top.

As new layers of sediment form, they press down on the older layers beneath them. This pressure forces out the water between the sediment in the older layers. Chemicals in the water form crystals. As the crystals grow, they glue the older pieces of sediment together. This forms new sedimentary rock. Layers of sedimentary rock are called strata.

CARVING OUT LANDFORMS

Weathering and erosion help form rock by making sediment. However, they also break down the rocks on Earth's surface over time. This slow cycle of making and breaking down rock creates many interesting landforms. These landforms include cliffs, plateaus, and the rock arches of the United States' western deserts.

The Landscape Arch, in Arches National Park, Utah, is the longest natural rock arch in the world!

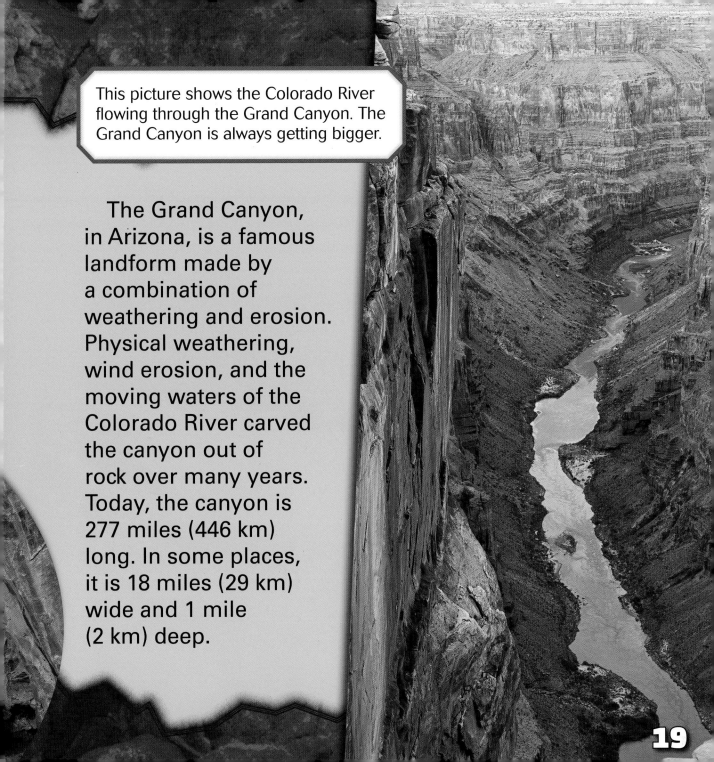

This picture shows the Colorado River flowing through the Grand Canyon. The Grand Canyon is always getting bigger.

The Grand Canyon, in Arizona, is a famous landform made by a combination of weathering and erosion. Physical weathering, wind erosion, and the moving waters of the Colorado River carved the canyon out of rock over many years. Today, the canyon is 277 miles (446 km) long. In some places, it is 18 miles (29 km) wide and 1 mile (2 km) deep.

CAUSING PROBLEMS FOR PEOPLE

Erosion and weathering are at work in many of Earth's **natural disasters**. For example, gravity pulls loose sediment, mud, and snow downhill. Large amounts of sediment, mud, or snow moving downhill very quickly can cause landslides, mudslides, and avalanches.

This picture shows an avalanche in the Alps, a mountain range in Europe. The winter of 1950 to 1951 is known as the Winter of Terror because 649 avalanches happened in the Alps that winter.

When these buildings were built, they were not this close to the edge of the cliff. Weathering and erosion have worn the cliff away over hundreds of years.

Beach erosion can cause flooding in coastal areas. Beaches normally create a barrier between the ocean and coastal land. When beaches are eroded, this barrier is removed. During a storm or hurricane, coastal areas may flood when ocean waters rise quickly during a storm. Storm waves and currents can also quickly erode beaches even more. Erosion caused by a storm may make coastal flooding even more likely during the next storm.

PART OF THE CYCLE

Weathering and erosion help create sedimentary rock. However, other kinds of rocks are created by Earth's rock cycle as well. These are metamorphic rock and igneous rock.

The rock cycle is Earth's process of breaking down old rock and forming new rock. Any kind of rock can become any other kind of rock!

Over time, weathering and erosion **expose** rocks found below Earth's surface. Once these rocks reach Earth's surface, weathering and erosion will break them down. The rock cycle never ends!

Jasper National Park, in Alberta, Canada, has mountains, lakes, waterfalls, and glaciers.

GLOSSARY

absorb (ub-SORB) To take in and hold on to something.

chemical (KEH-mih-kul) Matter that can be mixed with other matter to cause changes.

continents (KON-tuh-nents) Earth's seven large landmasses.

deposited (dih-PAH-zuht-ed) Left behind.

dissolved (dih-ZOLVD) Broke down.

expand (ek-SPAND) To spread out or to grow larger.

expose (ik-SPOHZ) To put in plain sight.

gravity (GRA-vih-tee) The natural force that causes objects to move toward the center of Earth.

grind (GRYND) To crush into tiny pieces.

landforms (LAND-formz) Features on Earth's surface, such as hills or valleys.

microscopic (my-kreh-SKAH-pik) Very small.

mineral (MIN-rul) Natural matter that is not an animal, a plant, or another living thing.

natural disasters (NA-chuh-rul dih-ZAS-terz) Major events caused by Earth's natural processes that often cause harm to people and property.

particles (PAR-tih-kulz) Small pieces of matter.

reacts (ree-AKTS) Causes a chemical change.

INDEX

WEBSITES

Due to the changing nature of Internet links, PowerKids Press has developed an online list of websites related to the subject of this book. This site is updated regularly. Please use this link to access the list:
www.powerkidslinks.com/rthf/erosi